My Little Black "A" Book
Communication Acronyms

Effective Communication in a Noisy World

Major Lynette Jones

Copyright © 2018 Major Lynette Jones
All rights reserved.

ISBN: 9781980938262

This book is dedicated to my late mother Shirley Ann Farris
she had a way with words.

My Little Black "A" Book Communication Acronyms

Effective Communication in a Noisy World

We live in a noisy world and this book is a quick guide to effectively help you communicate with others. My hope is that it will help you to question, examine, and think about the ways you listen and speak. This is My Little Black Acronym Book.

Major Lynette Jones

My Little Black "A" Book
Communication Acronyms

INTRODUCTION

Effective Communication in a
Noisy World

Written by Major Lynette Jones

As I grew up, my mother would always say things that I considered to be very harsh. She had a way with words and she was never afraid to tell people how she really felt and what she really thought. I remember that my mom would curse people out. She would even invent new curse words that I had never heard of before. I used to tell her that you can't say everything you want to say to people and you can't talk to me that way. She said, "Yes I can because I am a mother." I've always disagreed with that statement. As I grew up I saw my mother get into so many arguments with her male and female friends and even family members.

No one deserves to be cursed out. I totally disagreed with my mom. I even stopped speaking to her for a period of three months, because of the way that she spoke to me. It hurt my heart to do that and I guess I was trying to teach her a lesson. I believe that she learned a lesson because after I called her up, she started to cry and she said; "Lynette what can I do to get along with you? I love you so much." My response, "mom, you can't talk to me any kind of way. You have to respect me. I am an adult and I deserve that and I also demand it." "Just because you're a mother does not give you the right to say whatever you want to say to me." She even cursed out my aunt and they did not speak to each other for two years. Sadly to say, my mother passed away and they still were not speaking.

Before my mom died, I promised myself that I would never curse anyone out and that I will always try to communicate with people in a respectful decent manner. I must say that my mother slowed down in her old age, but no matter how old she got, she still had a way of communicating with people. I guess that was just her style. I loved my mother and I do miss her despite some of her words. She would definitely tell you what she thought. I got that part of her DNA!

My goal in life is to let people know they have a voice and they can talk to me, and that I would never curse them out or belittle them in any way. I will hang up the phone before I talk badly to another person. Yes, I may raise my voice and I may even get a little excited, but I would never curse anyone. My goal in life is not to put down, but to encourage. This book will help you to think about the ways in which you communicate and listen to other people. I hope that it helps you because it's definitely helping me.

The military has always used acronyms in order to abbreviate communication and help people remember things that are important and essential for future mental recall and reference. Using acronyms makes things easier to retain and immediately remember when there is a need to pull up the information quickly in conversations, meetings, and briefings. Sometimes short, sweet and to the point, sentences can be effective. Let me give you an example.

Acronym Sentence:

I have to get my **OER** before I **PCS**. I also have to update my **DA** photo in order to be considered for the next **APL**.

What does that mean to you? Well, if you are a military person, more specifically an Army Soldier then you do not need an explanation. If you are a civilian then you should feel lost right about now and there is nothing wrong with being lost. You just need someone to explain the acronym and then you will see the light.

Acronym Sentence Explained:

I have to get my "**Officer Evaluation Report**" (OER) before I "**Permanently Change Stations**" (PCS). I also have to update my "**Department of the Army**" (DA) photo in order to be considered for the next "**Army Promotion List**" (APL).

Acronyms are most effective when used in an organization where the majority of the audience is familiar with the terms and can relate to what you are saying. In the military, most people are required to learn the acronyms, as it is guaranteed that they will need to use most of them for their day-to-day duties and responsibilities.

What about those people who are not in the military? Well, in business and non-profit organizations, acronyms have become increasingly popular and helpful when it comes to educating and communicating to a group that is always coming up with programs and ideas that will be constantly repeated and discussed on a frequent basis. This short little book will be full of acronyms and I promise to translate them all to you. These are some life acronyms that I have put together to help you communicate in this noisy world in which we currently live.

One of the most innovative and sophisticated inventions of the 20th Century is the cell phone. How did we make it prior to 1981 without cell phones? I am still trying to get it… okay, moving on. The cell phone has replaced traveling for the purpose of a face-to-face meeting with people you know. No need to meet someone in person when you can just pick up your cell phone and have the same conversation via cellular technology. The point I am trying to make is that cell phones are good forms of communication; however, the rule of "old school" says there is nothing like a face-to-face conversation that provides clarity, no weak signal, no dropped calls and very little room for outside distractions.

I can't leave out e-mails as this is one of my favorites. Not only can I communicate with you, I don't even have to hear your voice. I just have to type and press send and I don't even have to wait for an immediate response. In my opinion, this is so impersonal, cold and empty. It might be okay if you are not a people person. Don't get me wrong emails are good in their place but they are not good for warm, personal, effective communication.

Today there are so many different ways to communicate and get our points across. In this book, I want to give you some acronyms to create short precise communication that may help you in your everyday business and social conversations. How do you know the things you know in life? Somebody had to teach you, so please get ready to learn, the acronym teacher is here! Most of the time when we are having a conversation with someone and they mention an acronym we may ask them "What does that mean?" Most of the time people don't have a problem explaining to us what it means.

Conversation is all about quality. Trust me, when you open your mouth it only takes a few moments before a person can tell a lot about you. In just that brief moment of time, please make it count. Your communication should be of value. One dollar has value but it's not worth much at an upscale restaurant. $100 has value and you may be able to have a nice dinner and dessert at the same upscale restaurant. Put a value on your communication. Let people know you are worth the conversation.

You can improve your communication skills if you are willing to work at it. How do you do that? You take the time to learn and fit into that environment. This book will educate you and provoke thought. I hope it will help you become a precise and effective communicator. Read and learn. **(RAL)**

What is noise? The definition of noise is a sound, especially one that is loud or unpleasant or that causes a disturbance. The focus for the purpose of this book is the noise that causes a disturbance. We really do live in a noisy world and that sometimes makes it hard to communicate with each other. Communication skills are something that we have to truly work at in order to become effective. Communication noise can be past history, cultural background, literal noise, and verbal/body language. These things impact the message. Our communication is not as clear-cut as we may want it to be. How can we clear up this noise? It's a process of elimination. Get out of the past, learn other cultures, choose a quiet place to talk and check your body language. Okay, this takes practice but you can do it. Always think win-win when you engage in any form of communication.

Identify and list seven ways you can improve your communication skills this week.

1. _____
2. _____
3. _____
4. _____
5. _____
6. _____
7. _____

Effective Communication

Table of Contents

Communicate – Collaborate – Commit 9
"Why Am I Talking" 13
"Bottom Line Up Front" 15
Speak Educate Excite 17
Just Listen and Shut Up 19
Always Listen First 21
Communicate Under Trust 23
Don't Interrupt People 25
Listen to Opinions 27
Pay Attention to a Person's Body Language 28
Don't Argue With a Client 29
Call Don't Text 31
It's Not About Me 33
Learn From Others 35
Listen With Your Heart 37
You Learn By Listening 39
Don't Assume You Know the Outcome 41
Communication Rules Of Engagement 43
Everyone Doesn't Know You 44
Let Other People Talk 46
Network with Strangers 48
Toxic Communication Stinks 50
Have One Conversation at a Time 52

Don't Lie To People 54
Pay Attention to Details 56
Always Practice Your Communication Skills 57
ACRONYM REFERENCES 59

CCC

Communicate – Collaborate – Commit
"The Three C's of Communication"

This entire book is about communication and different acronyms that help us to look at effective ways to communicate. So how does a person communicate effectively? It starts with transferring information from one entity to another. There is something that you want to make known or to bring to someone's attention. Communication is the interchanging of thoughts, opinion, or information. There are a few forms of communication: written, verbal and non-verbal, and physical communication can also be put into the mix. In today's world, one of the most popular forms of communicating is through text messaging. This is one of the most convenient ways of communicating quick, fast and in a hurry. Does anyone remember pagers? I remember people saying "page me" because they thought they were so important! Now they say "text me"! We went from a "P" to a "T" moving up the alphabet. This is just an introduction to provoking thought as it relates to communication.

Communicate, collaborate and commit are three baselines I would like to use in this section. These are anchors to communicating in various organizations. We can integrate the "Three C's" into just about every conversation, we have.

When we open our mouth that is communication so we communicate. During a conversation, we agree or pledge to do something either at that time or at a later time that is committing. Once we commit to the thing we have committed to, we then work with others to achieve a common goal. That is collaboration.

Let's look at the word communicate. There are three components of communication **verbal, nonverbal and communication guidelines**. Let's look at verbal communication. When you have a verbal conversation you should always clarify your words, have good listening skills, voice quality, and volume. When you are talking to someone the most important thing is clarity of words. Make sure you are clear and concise when you are explaining something to another person. People like to have a clear understanding and one of the ways they can do that is through clarity. Have you ever walked away from a meeting not sure of what someone has said? It's not a bad idea to ask the person giving the information to clarify things for you. It's important that you understand the information that is being given to you.

Listening skills are just as important as **verbal communication** skills. They actually go hand in hand. If you listened to a presentation and you walked away with the same feeling as someone who wasn't even there, you might as well not have heard it at all. Listening can open up a world of understanding and clarity and give you fuel to move forward on your journey of becoming an effective communicator. Voice quality is also important. Have you ever attended an information briefing and the quality of the person's voice was low and you couldn't hear them very well?

The Three C's of Communication

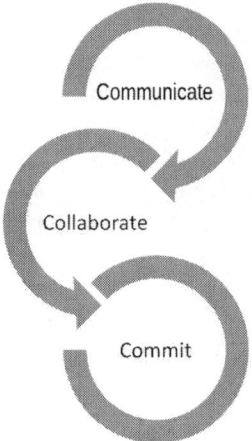

It's like you are straining to hear them which is a communication barrier. Not speaking clearly, not listening and not having voice quality is like not hearing anything at all. This also includes volume, it's like a busted speaker, turn it off. Volume comes into play when you are speaking in a place where you don't have a microphone. Volume is important and one of the most annoying things is when you are attending a speaking engagement and someone yells, "I can't hear you"! Now you find yourself wanting to yell in order to be heard, but that only puts a strain on your vocal cords. Learning to incorporate all the factors into your communication can be challenging but it's not impossible.

Nonverbal communication: 90% of communication is nonverbal, when nonverbal communication does not match verbal language, miscommunication can happen. People make assumptions based on nonverbal communication. Sometimes your tone of voice affects how you are heard. You didn't say that you were angry but the urgency, hesitancy and belligerent tone of your voice might suggest that you are angry or upset. Body language is another cue. Some people fold their arms, lean forward or become fidgety. What is that saying? Well, you have to take a guess, because it's nonverbal communication. Facial Expressions such as looking disinterested, apprehensive or frowning can tell a whole lot about how you may be feeling. When I was a teenager people use to say, "Why do you look so mean?" I had to defend myself quite often by telling them, "I am not mad, I just look that way!" I had to change my outlook.

Communication guidelines are things we have to own up to. We can't always blame other people for the way we communicate and the way they see us. Sometimes people only judge you by the way you look. If you look clean, people will label you clean. If you look dirty it works the same way. You could be clean when in fact you are really dirty. A few communication guidelines, own your feelings by using "I" statements, avoid generalizations like always, never and everyone. Take responsibility for how you feel, describe a behavior or situation rather than being judgmental. Be specific rather than general.

Communication leads to **Collaboration.** It's important to foster an environment of trust. It's so hard to operate, let alone work with someone you don't trust. I could write another book on trust alone. There are so many different levels of trust, but this type of trust comes when you are collaborating with someone. If you are going to collaborate with people you have to realize that different styles are valued, people have to communicate respectfully and differences have to be dealt with early. Collaboration is something you do with others and not something you do alone. You have to see teammates as collaborators, not competitors. You have to be supportive, not suspicious when you collaborate with others. Focus on the team and not on yourself. You can get a lot done and move ahead a lot faster when you collaborate with others. It is a part of communication.

Commitment is the key that holds it all together. Think about marriage and the phrase, "till death do us part." Think of how many marriages would last if people were more committed. Commitment usually is discovered in the midst of adversity. Always clarify your values and goals. Commitment comes as the result of choice, not conditions. Commitment lasts when it is based on values. One way to improve your commitment is to tie your commitments to your values. Take a risk.

Identify and list seven people you will communicate, collaborate and commit to this week.

1. _____
2. _____
3. _____
4. _____
5. _____
6. _____
7. _____

Note to Self:

_____
_____
_____
_____
_____
_____

CHAPTER ONE

WAIT

"Why Am I Talking"

Some people just talk too much. This is just real, not rude, but real. In my short little lifetime, I have heard people talk about things and people. It is of no benefit to anyone and it's not even uplifting or encouraging to those who are recipients of the conversation. I call it a meaningless conversation, why am I talking? "WAIT!" I am going old school for a moment or two. When you open your mouth to say something it should be seasoned with salt. It should be for the good of the order and it should be something that will edify those around you; those who have given you the time and energy to listen! Every single time I open my mouth, I want it to be for the good of someone who is listening to me. This is my moment to make or break, shake or take.

I remember when my mother was alive she would tell you exactly what she thought, no matter if it was good or bad, happy or sad. Her tongue was so sharp that she cut me a couple of times with it, and I had to stitch up my own wounds. There was no time to go to the hospital; I would not have made it to the emergency room. There was a rhyme that was said when I was a little girl. Some of you may know it or maybe even have heard it; "*Sticks and stones may break my bones but names will never hurt me.*" Some crazy adult taught that to some innocent kid and the rest is history. If you think that sticks and stones may break your bones than you are right. If you think that names will never hurt you, then you are wrong. I must admit I really don't care what people think about me. If they call me a name naturally that hurts me whether it's true or not. Bad names and slander can cut a person to the core. So my advice in this chapter is to "**Wait**" before you put your tongue in motion. We should use our tongue to build up and not tear down. In the good book, it says that the tongue is a restless evil. We should not use it to cruse but to praise. Examine why you are talking, whom you are talking to, and what is the purpose of you talking. This may keep you out of trouble.

Some people think that just because they have two lips and a tongue that they always have to use it. Okay, there is something called the First Amendment to the Constitution and we have a right to exercise it. When you do decide to exercise it, then you should have something meaningful and purposeful to say. Use it to build people up and not tear them down. Why am I talking, because I care about you because I want to give you some good information because I want to help you because I want to warn you about something that may cause you harm? Always ask yourself and remember this chapter title, "WAIT"

Identify and list seven people you will talk to and ask WAIT this week. (Use the WAIT acronym)

1. _____
2. _____
3. _____
4. _____
5. _____
6. _____
7. _____

Why Am I Talking

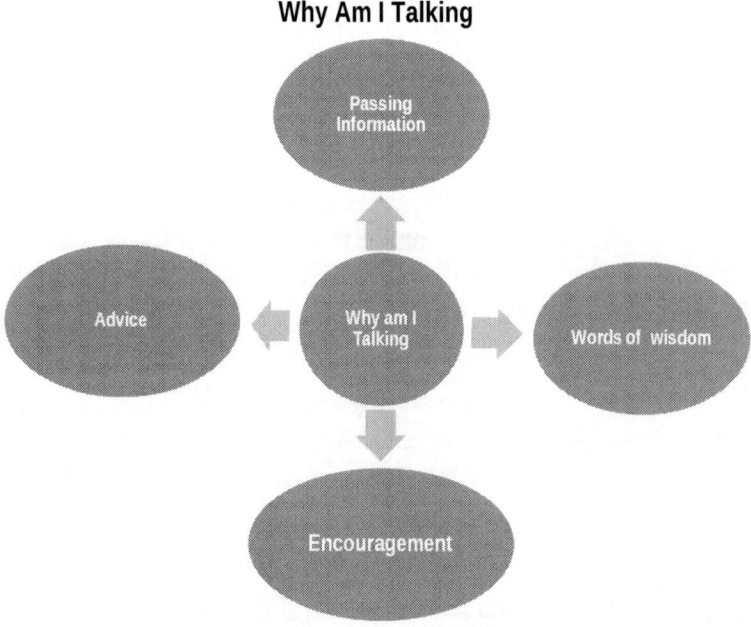

CHAPTER TWO

BLUF

"Bottom Line Up Front"

What is it you want to say without going to Egypt and back? In this beautiful world, we live in, I have come to realize that people like to talk and some people like to talk more than others. I believe in the power of storytelling, but when it comes to business I don't have time to tell a story. I only have time to make my point in order for a decision to be made. There are times in our life when we have to tell people the Bottom Line Up Front, the **"BLUF**!" This is definitely a military expression. There are times in the military when we have to brief higher officials. I remember times when I was in Afghanistan and I had to prepare a brief for a two-star general officer. I spent hours preparing for this particular brief and I had my talking points all laid out. I wanted to explain to the General the back-story as to why I arrived at my decision and the reason he should go with my recommendation. The big day came and I was ready. When it was my turn to brief, I was prepared to give him a detailed answer. "What's the BLUF?" That is all he wanted to know. Really Sir? This was my time to sound extra intelligent and show him what I had. The only thing he wanted was the BLUF. Sometimes we all want to be heard and we want to show our passion for the things we are passionate about, but we also have to learn to be brief and be done. This doesn't mean that we won't get to tell our story; it just means that our story will have to tell itself at another place and time. We have to always be able to adjust and accept that not everyone we talk to cares about the story. They just want to get to the ending. Always come with the end in mind. Keep it short, simple and not long and lengthy. Hit all your major points in the shortest time possible.

Let me clarify there is nothing wrong with explaining yourself or a situation to someone. There is nothing wrong with taking a certain amount of time to do so. The point in this chapter is that sometimes people just want you to get to the point. I have seen it time and time again. People will not tell you that you talk too much, but they will tell someone else that you talk too much and that they just want the BLUF. Most people are polite when it comes to tolerating people when they are communicating.

I remember being with Congresswoman Maxine Waters and one of her constituents approached her. She was on her feet all day and the event was almost over. A man approached her and he starting telling her about a problem he was having in his community. He went on and on and on. She patiently stood there and listened to him. After he said all he had to say, she said, "give me your name and number and I will look into the matter." The whole time I was thinking, "man just get to the point." I guess that's why I am not the congresswoman. The point is she didn't mind listening to him, but it would have been less time spent if he had just gotten to the point. Time is important. I think we should spend our time and conversation wisely.

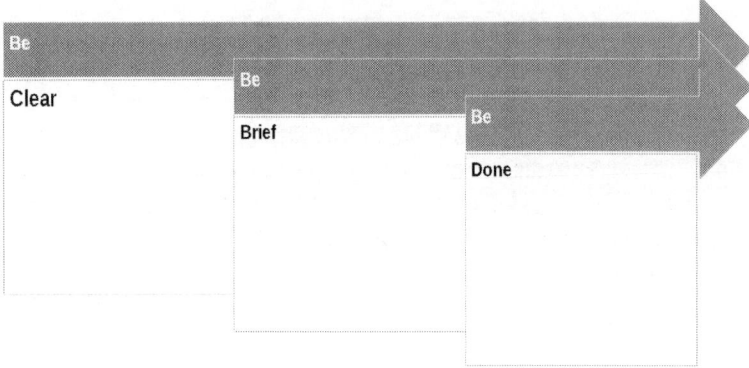

CHAPTER THREE
SEE
Speak Educate Excite

Let's face it; talking is an everyday part of life. It is a necessary function that most people will exercise until the day they die. I am a firm believer that when you speak to people about life and business matters you should speak to educate and excite them to take action. When you are in a situation where you are trying to close a deal, you have to educate your potential client on the product or service you are trying to sell to them. Once you educate them, you should get them excited about why they are doing business with you in the first place.

When you are trying to tell your teenage daughter about sex, you should educate her on what will happen if she has sex and the consequences that could follow her choice. Then you get her excited about how it's better to be old-fashioned and wait until she is married. This is what you have accomplished: you have spoken to her, you have educated her and hopefully you have gotten her excited about not becoming a mother at a young age. There was a lady at the church I attend, who wanted me to talk to her granddaughter about joining the military. When I spoke to her I had to educate her on the ways of the military, my experience and the expectation of being a Soldier. I got her excited based on my experience coupled with the adventures and rewards of being in the military. She got excited, because I employed the acronym, "**SEE**."

One key point is to be efficient when you are speaking. Even if the young lady never joins the military, I was able to at least give her a glimmer of hope and she had a positive baseline to reference. I know some people who have personally told me that they would never recommend the military to their daughters, because of some negative and unfortunate circumstances they experienced. We all have experiences that are not good, I know that sounds elementary, but if you can't speak to educate and excite then don't work to destroy and discourage. Life is worth the living so live it! Try to educate and excite people along the way. Life is like a vapor that appears for a little while and then it vanishes away. You don't have much time, so start getting people excited through conversation! They say you only have one time to make a first impression but you can always get a second opinion.

Identify and list four people you will SEE this week. (Based on the acronym)
1. _____
2. _____
3. _____
4. _____

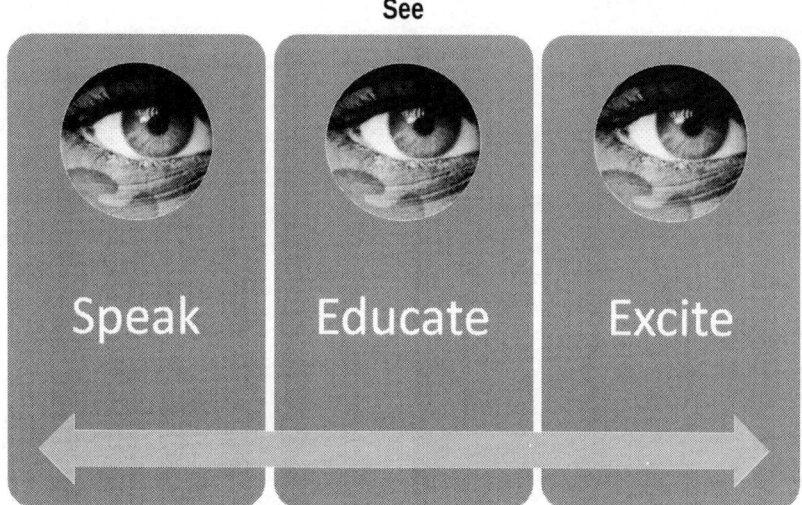

CHAPTER FOUR

JLASU

Just Listen and Shut Up

Most people get mad when you tell them to shut up. Okay, I will be the first to admit that telling someone to shut up is just plain rude. What if you tell yourself to shut up and listen? Wow, it got quiet! Sometimes that's exactly what you have to do when someone wants you to listen to them without any comments. This can in most cases be hard for some of us to do. My Godmother has the gift to listen. I call her quite often and we talk for hours. Okay, I talk for hours and she just listens without saying a word. I sometimes think to myself maybe she fell asleep. On several occasions, I have sat and talked to her in person. She sits there intently listening to me while taking mental notes. This is a gift that most of us could afford to learn and use in our everyday life, in order to improve our listening skills. My Godmother has set the example for me, so I try to use it every time someone comes to me and wants to talk. I just listen and shut up. I know how to talk and respond, I think I am pretty good at it, but I can always be a better listener. When you add silence to your conversation you can learn a whole lot. I have learned that sometimes people just want to be heard they need a sounding board, an outlet without sound. Most people are just trying to work some things out psychologically, and they just need to hear themselves talk out loud. They value a person who can just listen and not judge. There is an expression that the older folks say, "It is better to be seen and not heard" this is true sometimes. Practice being seen by the person who is talking to you, as being a good, sound listener. Listening is a talent and acts as a gift at the same time. Rewind for just a moment, I want to clarify an acronym from the BLUF chapter in order to avoid any contradictions. When you are doing business with others or attending meetings you should use the BLUF method. When you are dealing with people who are near and dear to your heart, then you should just listen and shut up, because they want and need to be heard.

    Certain non-verbal communication demonstrates exposure to certain rules and environments in which that rule lives. One of the most important things in communication is hearing what is not said. I didn't hear you say you love me, but you're actions spoke louder than your words. You didn't wish me a speedy recovery, but you came to the hospital to visit me every other day. Sometimes we can smash a person for the things we wish they would say when they don't say them to us. Actions speak louder than words so silence your tongue and just listen.

Identify and meet with three people you will just shut up and listen to this week.

1. _____
2. _____
3. _____

Just Listen and Shut Up

Pause → **Silence** → **Quiet** → **Listen** → **Shut up** → (Pause)

CHAPTER FIVE
ALF
Always Listen First

In a common sense approach, it's always better to listen first and then speak. Take a moment to think about how many people don't listen before they speak and find their foot in their mouth. Information is gathered by listening first so that you can obtain a clear understanding of the information given. I believe listening is an art, talent, and skill that not everyone possesses. During my early days in the military, I was assigned to conduct investigations. They were called 15-6 investigations. When there was something that the Army wanted to investigate they would assign an officer to gather all the facts and interview those involved. This taught me to be an active listener. I had to gather and listen to so many people and my opinion and thoughts were not important until the investigation was completed. I could not even come to my own conclusion until I heard everyone's side of the story. This was a challenge for me because I like to talk. When we find ourselves in certain situations where we have to listen and not speak, we should take full advantage of grabbing this skill and putting it in our life tool bag. Always listen first, you might learn something and save yourself a little embarrassment.

    Okay, another true story. I was invited to be a part of the Rose Parade and ride on one of the floats. Being in the military caused this to be a challenge for me, but I worked it out. I had to get permission from the higher powers to be in order to participate. I promise I did everything I was supposed to do and I got permission to ride on the float. I was good to go. Well, this thing called gossip got into the mix and someone told my supervisor that I did not follow protocol and that I was not following orders. Okay, this is where it gets good. My supervisor called me and before I could speak, he ripped me up and down and down and up. I have tough skin. I survived this verbal attack. I tried to explain to my supervisor that I took all the right steps and got permission. My supervisor didn't want to listen and told me that I should be quiet and learn to listen. Amazing! I couldn't even open my mouth and explain the facts. In the end, I was in the parade and I didn't go to jail or get kicked out of the military for riding on a float, imagine that! During that butt chewing session, I realized that it's always better is listen, gather the facts and then speak. Communication is not a one-way street. My supervisor took away my voice. The only person my supervisor should have listened to was me and not a jealous third party. Always listen first.

Identify and list three people you will just listen to before you give a verbal response.

1. _____
2. _____
3. _____

Always Listen First

- Receive the information
- Process the information
- Respond to the information you received and processed

CHAPTER SIX

CUT

Communicate Under Trust

How do you know that when you talk to someone and tell them something personal and confidential, they are not going to repeat it? One thing that I have seen and witnessed with my own eyeballs is people running their mouth telling other people's business. Shame! When I was a kid I had a nickname they called me Rona Barrett. I got that name because I had a habit of running back and repeating things. I was a kid! What did I know? When someone told me something, I couldn't wait to tell it to someone else. Thank God I grew up and now I know what it means for someone to talk to me in confidence. I have learned not to repeat a matter. I feel that if a person wants the world to know about things they tell you in secret, then they should just get on the bullhorn and repeat it to the whole world!

    I remember when I was a captain in the Army and had a supervisor who was not trustworthy. Yes, another supervisor story. I had some problems with him; we didn't seem to get along. One day in private he told me to tell him what I really thought and that I could trust him. He said let's air out our differences. Little did I know at the time this would be a big mistake. I told him how I felt. After I was done he said, and I quote, "thank you for being honest with me, I appreciate it. Now we can start with a clean slate." One week later he calls me into his office with another soldier present. He counseled me and wrote me up. Everything I told him in private he annotated on the counseling statement. That was one of the biggest acts of betrayal to me and at that moment I knew that I could not trust him and that I would never tell him anything ever again. He violated my communication under trust, my "CUT." Most people I trust, I don't have to tell them to keep it confidential. People feel good when they know they can trust you.

    At this point in my life, I only have private conversations with people I trust. If I can't trust you with my personal information then I don't even talk about it. One thing that used to push my buttons is when I told a member of my family something and they went back and repeated it to another family member. If I wanted the whole family to know then I would have called a family reunion and made a public announcement. There are personal and private things about us that we don't want everyone to know. Even if it sounds like nothing to you, it matters to the person who told you. Let people know they can trust you when they communicate with you.

Identify and list three people you will talk to and not tell anyone else what you talked about this week.

1. _____
2. _____
3. _____

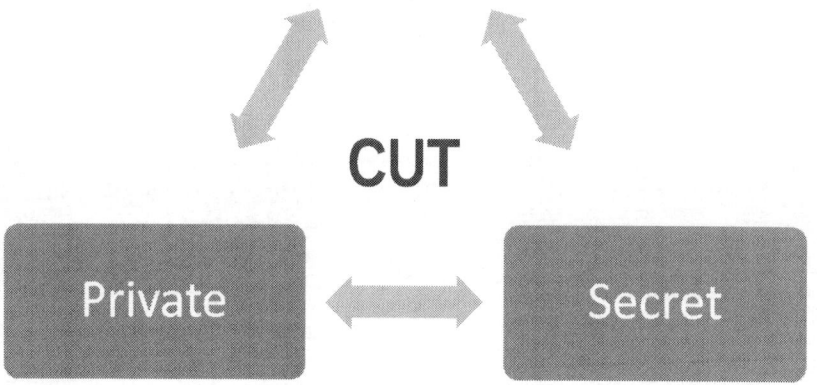

CHAPTER SEVEN

DIP

Don't Interrupt People

I must say I am guilty of interrupting people sometimes during a conversation. I could spend all day on this chapter alone. This is horrible, and I know so many other people who do the same thing. Usually, you interrupt someone when you really want to make a point or an argument is about to happen. If you really think about it, it is a very selfish act. I don't want to hear what you have to say; I just want to get my point across. That is the bottom line no sugarcoating here. The best rule of thumb is to not interrupt a person while they are talking. It is just rude; there is no other word to describe it.

    I remember when I had to fire an independent contractor over the phone. The first thing I said was, "please tell me what's on your mind and I will listen and not interrupt you." "When I speak I expect the same courtesy." Well, that didn't happen. The contractor spoke and I listened. Shortly after I started to talk, the contractor interrupted me. I got cut off and the contractor told me off! I guess you can say that I had an off day. When the conversation started to escalate even though I do not like to hang up on people, in this case, it was necessary. I said I wish you well and I'll talk to you later and I hung up. One thing I have learned in my little short life is if I am paying my cell phone bill, I have the right to talk to whomever I want to and I don't have to listen to anyone tell me off. Sometimes our emotions get the best of us and sometimes we don't want to hear what the other person has to say. This is where self-control comes in. Even if you don't want to hear what is being said, you have to learn how to listen. Life is not a one-sided journey it is a two-way street. The next time you are having a conversation with someone and the conversation is not going the way you want it to just "**DIP**." Don't interrupt people.

Identify and list seven people you will not interrupt this week.

1. _____
2. _____
3. _____
4. _____
5. _____
6. _____
7. _____

Don't Interrupt People

It's Rude!

CHAPTER EIGHT

LTO

Listen to Opinions

How many great ideas are there in the world today? How many times have we ignored someone's opinion and how many times have we had our own opinions ignored? We have to know the difference between an opinion and a fact. Okay, this sounds elementary, but the fact is that your opinion is a view or judgment formed about something, not necessarily based on fact or knowledge. Where is the education when you ask someone for their opinion? We can get bad advice from good people, but we usually don't get bad advice from experienced people. It can happen, but in most cases, it doesn't happen too often.

Here comes the common sense factor. I am not a mother. I have no biological children, so when one of my closest friends wanted to give me advise on motherhood and she didn't have any children of her own, it was hard to take her advice. What did she know about being a mother? It was her opinion and she felt she could give me advice because of our friendship and not because of her experience. Yes, this is common sense, too easy. Here is another example; I have been a businesswoman for approximately 25 years. A friend told me that she was starting her own business. She never asked for my opinion. She launched her business and was on her way. We had a few conversations about the business and I wanted to hear her business strategies. The whole time she was talking to me I just shook my head and my internal conversation went something like this. "What are you doing? "What are you saying?" You don't get it." I don't think by any means that I am the small business expert; I just have 25 years of experience. Experience is a good teacher it takes someone like me to know.

Finally, when she was done talking I gave her my opinion; I didn't put down her ideas. I just offered some suggestions. This was not a hunting trip; I wasn't looking to shoot her down. The decision was hers to make. My intentions were purely attached to her success and that is where my opinion was formulated. If you have people in your life that have your back and who have experience in an area that affects you, then listen to their advice, weigh it and then make your decision.

Identify and list four people you will give your opinion to this week.

1. _____
2. _____
3. _____
4. _____

CHAPTER NINE
PATAPBL

Pay Attention to a Person's Body Language

How many different languages do you speak? Body language is the process of communicating nonverbally through conscious or unconscious gestures and movements. You can find out a lot of things about a person based on their body language. It can be physical behavior such as facial expressions, body posture, gestures, eye movement, touch and the use of space. News flash, body language is not sign language don't get it confused. In the world of business, we have meetings on a regular basis. Sometimes we learn and or come to certain conclusions about people based on their body language.

When we are communicating with people we should hone in on their body language. It will let us know if it's a good time to talk to them at that moment or if we should postpone until a later date. If a person's body language tells you that now is not a good time you should notice it. Let me give you an example. There was a very successful businessman who was at the airport in Los Angeles, he was trying to catch a flight, was late and in a hurry. He made it to his departure gate with five minutes to spare before boarding. There was another man in the airport that recognized him and took advantage of the moment and approached him. He introduced himself and wanted to talk business right then and there. Obviously, then and there was not the time. There were a lot of factors present and he simply didn't take notice.

First, the businessman was in a rush and very distracted. He only had five minutes until boarding and he had to pay attention to the boarding announcements. The man kept talking and the businessman kept looking toward the gate to see when boarding would actually begin. The businessman was trying to be diplomatic, but he was not in the mood for any conversation. The man kept rudely talking even though it was clear the businessman was distracted. Sometimes you have to pay attention to a person's body language. You don't have to know why that a person is distracted; you just have to see that they are. There is an expression in the military that says, pay attention to details and body language is a detail.

Sometimes I show up at my aunt's house unexpectedly. She never minds me coming over. There have been times when she was not feeling good. Recognizing this, I didn't want to stay any longer because I wanted her to get her rest. Her body language said, I want to lie down and relax and my common sense told me the same thing. I would leave in order to respect her body language. Pay attention to a person's body language. You could learn a lot just by doing so.

CHAPTER TEN

DAWAC

Don't Argue With a Client

One thing I have learned is that you cannot argue with everybody. There is a saying that the customer is always right. I must admit I do not agree with that at all. No man or woman is always right. How can a customer be right all the time? It's just a contradiction in my opinion. Well, even if the customer is wrong, it's a bad idea to argue with him or her. Clients are the backbone of your business, without them, you would have no business. This chapter will warrant two stories.

The first story is when I launched my radio station. I had a client who was already edgy, but she was a client. I really didn't care for her attitude, but she was a client. I'm not sure if I really liked her, but she was a client. One day we recorded a show and I made a few errors in the show and I fixed the errors. The client wanted the show with the errors and I refused to give it to her. I said I did some edits and here is the new and improved show. She insisted on having the show with the errors. I didn't want to give it to her so we went back-and-forth. I was arguing with my client! At that moment I knew she would not come back and she did not come back. I thought to myself, maybe I should have just given her a crappy product, but that's not in my nature. Then I asked myself why did she want the crappy product in the first place? In this case, maybe I should've given it to her, but that's not my style. That day I learned a lesson. No, it was not that the client was always right; sometimes you have to give up your right to be right.

In the next story, I was the client. There was a lady doing credit repair for me. I felt that she was not doing a good job, so I called her on it. The conversation was anything other than pleasant. After I confronted her, the conversation started to escalate. "Can I say something?" I asked her, "she said, "no I'm talking and you're listening I'm good at what I do, and you don't have the right to question me". It was only by the grace of God, that I didn't jump through the phone. Okay, it was also not humanly possible for me to do so. I had to take it and at that moment I learned another life lesson, qualify a person before you do business with them. Even though she was a referral from a friend, I don't blame the friend I blame the unprofessionalism of the provider. Don't argue with clients. It's unprofessional and it could cost you some money. Trust me she will never get a referral from me. That doesn't mean that I don't forgive her, it just means that I didn't forget.

Identify and list two people you avoided an argument with this week.
1. _____
2. _____

Don't Argue With a Client

CHAPTER ELEVEN

CDT

Call Don't Text

Text messaging is pretty convenient; sometimes you can just say hello without having a long conversation. Text messaging is good for a quick note or to have a non-verbal conversation. There are times when things need to be said, not typed no text. If you really need to talk to someone and get detailed information, do not send a text. Pick up the phone! I know that's easier said than done. For some people, conducting a phone conversation is challenging and can feel awkward. Practice is a good way to overcome your discomfort. Yours can be a legitimate discomfort, but please do try and get over it. It's good to work through difficult challenges. This is when it's time to grow up and make a phone call. Not to say you are juvenile because you text instead of calling. It's to say be an adult. You can't deliver the same intimate message through a text. A phone call shows that someone cares about you and is willing to give you their time and undivided attention just to share a conversation with you. So Call, don't Text!

Being a woman in business, I don't mind picking up a phone and calling a person, especially when there are challenges or when I have to deal with tough issues. I must admit though that I have used text messages as bait. When you throw a good piece of meat out there, you are bound to make a big catch. Sure, I have sent the most enthusiastic text messages to people. I could have just made the same effort to *call* and say the same things I said in the text message and perhaps garnered a response.

If you need to borrow money from someone perhaps you should call them and ask and not text. I have a few examples of this. A person, I know asked to borrow some money from me. The first time they asked, they called me on the phone and we talked about it and I agreed to loan them the money. By the grace of God, the person paid me back in a few months. A few months later they needed to borrow more money. Well, they did pay the first debt. However this time instead of calling me on the phone, they sent me a text message. If it's that important, pick up the phone and ask. I thought it was so impersonal to send a text message to ask for more money. I know people ask for money all the time via text. News flash, please don't ask me for money via text. If you have to ask, call. I don't need a long explanation or sad story; just a request and if my circumstances permit, I'll see what I can do.

Some things are just too important to communicate via a text message. Trust me, people will have more respect for you if you look them in the eye or call them on the phone. Text messaging is good for this day and age, however, there is still nothing like a good ole phone call. A conversation consists of a beginning, middle and an end. A text message is a digital message you can't hear. It has no emotional context. All you can do is read it.

CHAPTER TWELVE
INAM
It's Not About Me

There are some people in this world who think that they are the center of attention. I am sure if you stop to think about it, you could think of at least one person who fits this description. Some people are unilateral speakers and some listeners. It's all about what they have to say that matters when you talk to them. A big key to successful communication is taking yourself completely out of the equation and putting the focus on the person to whom you are talking. When I am trying to secure a new client for advertising and sponsorship, one of the first things that I ask the client is what do you need and what do you wish to get out of this? What do you expect from me? It's not the other way around. I want to do this for you and I want you to succeed. It's not about me it's about the vision and expectation of my potential client. We sit down together to figure out the best strategy in order to accomplish the mission. My radio show is the vehicle, I am the driver and my clients are my passengers. I carry them to the place they want to go and not where I want to take them.

    A dear friend of mine recently opened a fitness center. She tried to figure out a way to get people to her new fitness studio. We had a conversation about it and we came up with a game plan. She threw out some ideas and I followed her lead. She put on a spin class (cycling) I agreed to bring her 12 people since she had 12 bikes. We decided to do a spin class honoring Women's History Month. I had so many ideas and thoughts as to how we would carry this out. I had to stop a few times and tell myself, "This is not about you." I was present to help my friend in her new business. My role was to support her and get people to participate in the class. It was a successful ride and things went great. Just think if I had tried to inject all my ideas. I was there to help, not take over and lead the way. If I had done that then I would have been in the way. Once you get these four words in your head "IT'S NOT ABOUT ME" then you will start to realize that other people have something to say and they just might know more than you and they just might teach you something. There are approximately 7 billion people on this planet and you are just one of them. If your mind is always open, you will know that other people are valuable and special and that their opinions matter. Putting others before yourself is an act of courage and not a sign of weakness. Just remember it takes a pure heart to know that "It's not about me!"

Identify and list three people you put before yourself this week.
1. _____
2. _____
3. _____

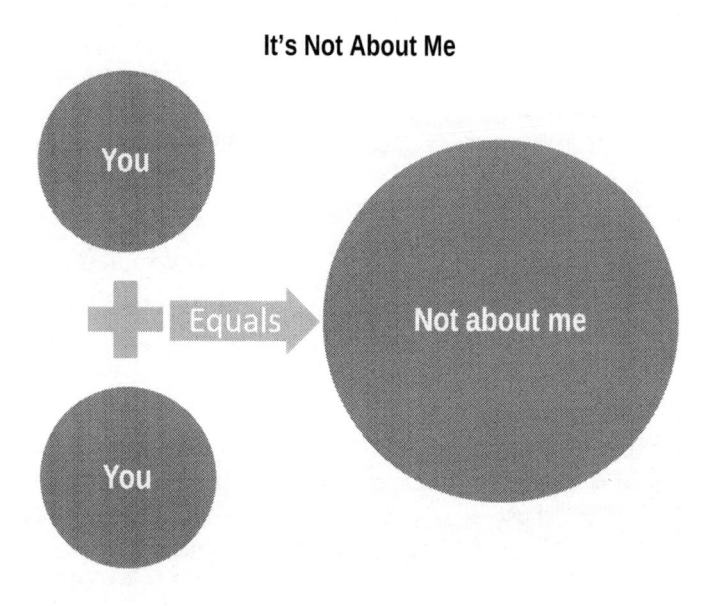

It's Not About Me

You + You Equals Not about me

CHAPTER THIRTEEN
LFO
Learn From Others

There have been times when I have been clueless in a situation. I really didn't know what was going on.

When I first began working at the United States Army Command (USARC), I had a very steep learning curve and I didn't know as much as I wanted to know. My job in the military is Human Resources and Logistics. There are times in a career when you don't always work in your field. Somewhere along the line, you will find yourself outside of your own system. In spite of having a vast knowledge of Army systems and computers in general, I found myself unable to navigate into the system required for my new job. I knew there were systems that would help me locate personal information on Soldiers. I didn't have access to the systems and I didn't know how to use it.

I know someone reading this can relate. At an early age in life, I learned to just listen and learn from others. By listening, you can learn what to do or what not to do. There used to be a commercial back in the day about test dummies that were placed in cars without their seatbelts. The voice on the commercial would always say, "You can learn a lot from a dummy!"

Well, that is the story of my life. I have learned a lot from people in general. In the last several months, I have had to learn a lot just by listening to people. The listening was not always someone speaking directly to me. It was from people in my environment talking about things that could impact me in some way. Since I was in learning mode, I had to always listen with my heart. There were and still are things that I just don't know, so I simply listen. I don't listen objectively or with doubt, I just let my heart take over and learn.

In my heart of hearts, I knew that I had to listen in order to learn and become good at my job. The heart is the beacon to most of our decision-making. Once you make up your mind to listen with your heart, things will start pumping and flowing a whole lot better. I was the new kid on the block and I didn't have room to try to be a know-it-all or a show-it-all. I know someone is saying that's how we learn, by watching other people. Yes, you are correct, but not everyone learns from others. Just know that common sense goes a long way.

Identify and list three people you learned from this week.

1. _____
2. _____
3. _____

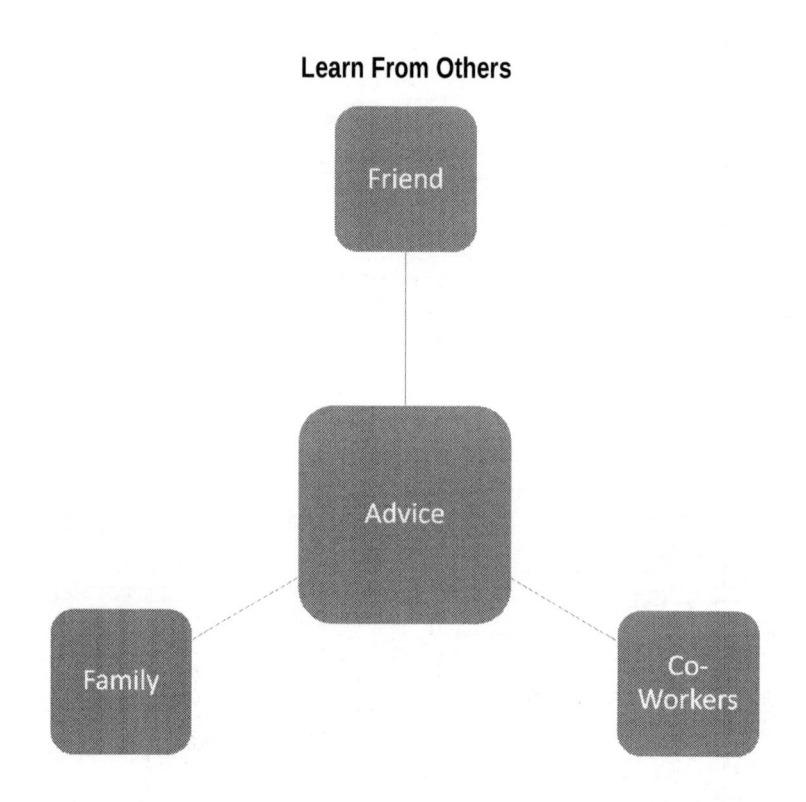

Learn From Others

- Friend
- Advice
- Family
- Co-Workers

CHAPTER FOURTEEN

LWYH

Listen With Your Heart

How do you listen to people when you are having a serious conversation with them? Do you listen in order to catch them in a lie? Do you listen in order to make them look stupid? Do you listen to them because you want to prove a point? Do you listen because you really want to hear what they have to say? Why do we listen to people? Most people already have the verdict on a person before they can even tell their story. How many juries reach a verdict before they hear the case being tried? In some cases, a jury can be deadlocked because of heart issues. Some people who sit on a jury trial feel in their hearts that the person on trial just might be innocent. Most of us are guilty of not listening with our hearts. How can we learn to listen with our heart? Look at people. Put away your phone, your IPad, and turn off the TV, computer, or anything else that may impede you from giving your attention to the person to whom you are talking. Stop what you are doing and give yourself over to the one who needs your listening ear, and your heart.

My twin sister is currently in South Korea. She was going through a situation and I was working on my book. I set a few hours aside on a Sunday afternoon after church to continue my writing. My phone rang and it was my sister. Her heart was heavy and she really needed a listening ear. At first, I tried to talk to her and write my book at the same time. At one point, I realized that she really needed my honest opinion about her situation and that I needed to just stop what I was doing and focus my complete attention on her. I can always write my book, however, I may not always be able to hear my sister's voice. She wanted to share with me and she wanted my feedback and didn't want to just be heard.

Sometimes in our lives, we have to realize that people are important and that we bring a lot to the table when we open up our hearts and listen to them. When you realize that matters of the heart are important and precious, then you will open up your heart every single time. Being a good listener also helps you to be a good communicator. Anyone can talk, but how well can you communicate your listening skills. Trust me when you are a good listener people will notice.

I don't listen objectively or with doubt, I just let my heart take over and learn. The heart is the beacon to most of our decision-making. As I've written before, once you make up in your mind to listen with your heart, things will start pumping and flowing a whole lot better.

Identify and list two people you will listen to with love this week.

1. _____
2. _____

Listen With Your Heart

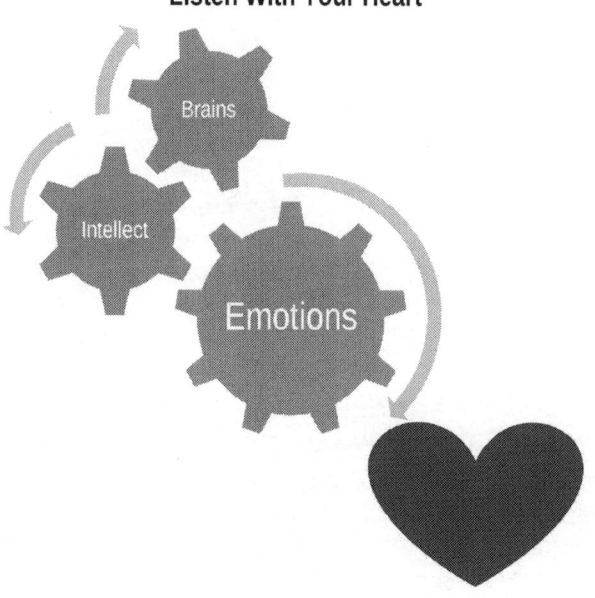

CHAPTER FIFTEEN

YLBL

You Learn By Listening

One thing I have come to learn in my life is that you can learn a lot just by listening to other people. I know there is a saying, "Monkey see, and Monkey do." Maybe there is some truth to that in the human sense. There have been times where I wanted to know something and I didn't want to ask anyone. I would just sit back, watch and listen and I can tell you that is when I have learned a lot about people.

There was a soldier at one of my units; she was miserable, you could tell because she tried to make everyone else miserable. Of course one of my questions was, "What's wrong with her, why is she like that?" Well, I could not go to her and ask her directly, we weren't exactly friends, and I don't even think we were acquaintances. As a matter of fact, I don't even think that we liked each other. I'm sure it was the latter! All you had to do was sit back, work, and listen to her conversations. She was loud, she was cocky, and she was miserable. I hate to say that I learned a lot about her personal life and her personal business just by listening. In this case, I really didn't want to hear it and yet I learned something. This may sound a little negative and I apologize for that. You can learn a lot about people and what to do and not do in certain situations just by listening.

I recently got stationed at Fort Bragg, North Carolina. I had to learn my job. I was in a new work environment. In some cases, I asked people what to do and at first, it seemed as though they didn't want to tell me. I had to listen to find out the order of things. I found myself interacting with a lot of people who are responsible for policy change. When there is a change in policy in the military, believe me, you have to listen. I got a chance to learn so much just by sitting in on briefings. Listening to other people's conversations, presentations and briefings helped me to communicate the things that I learned. I listen with intent. I can recall leaving meetings with other soldiers and they would say, "Did you get anything out of that meeting?" My reaction was, did YOU get anything out of that meeting? It just makes you realize that people don't listen in the same way that you do. This is not a put down it is a fact. Remember listening can also help you to be an effective communicator.

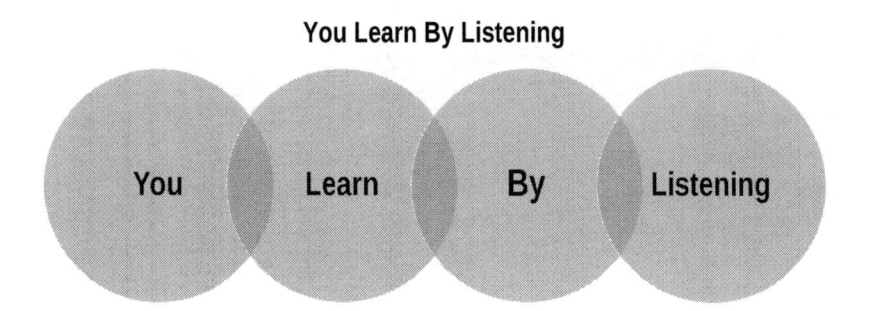

Identify and list four people you listened to this week.

1. _____
2. _____
3. _____
4. _____

You Learn By Listening

You — **Learn** — **By** — **Listening**

CHAPTER SIXTEEN
DAYKTO

Don't Assume You Know the Outcome

It's so easy to think that we know what's going on in someone else's head. It's no problem for us to imagine that we understand why a person has taken a particular course of action. We don't really know. We make a guess based on our imagination, experience or wishful thinking. It's not always good to assume you know the outcome of any situation unless it has already taken place. It is also no big deal for us to decide arbitrarily why people do what they do, or think how and what they think. Most of the time we don't make our decisions based on observable evidence or factual knowledge. We just make the decision and believe it as if it were true. The problem with making these types of assumptions, and we all do it, myself included, is that more often than not we are wrong. We assume that a person has a specific motivation for their actions or that an event took place, etc. We start to see these incorrect assumptions as gospel.

When you are communicating with someone, don't assume you know the outcome. I think that it is part of human nature to base our understanding on our experiences with other people and the world, not just the facts we observe. There are also our personal issues, which can attach to the process. Most of the time when I am talking to someone I have two conversations; the conversation I'm having with the person and the conversation that I am having in my own head. In most cases, this is a preconceived notion.

I have learned to listen and take notes and wait for the outcome because I only think I know, and sometimes I do, but sometimes I don't. One way is to just simply pause while we are jumping to our conclusion and say to ourselves, "I am not God so that means I don't know anything until it happens." We don't have the ability to know the future before it happens. Since we don't know, it would be wise to wait and listen. This will help us not to make assumptions. We don't know the outcome until it happens.

Identify and list six people that you assumed the outcome of their conversation and it was different this week.

1. _____
2. _____
3. _____
4. _____
5. _____
6. _____

Don't Assume You Know the Outcome

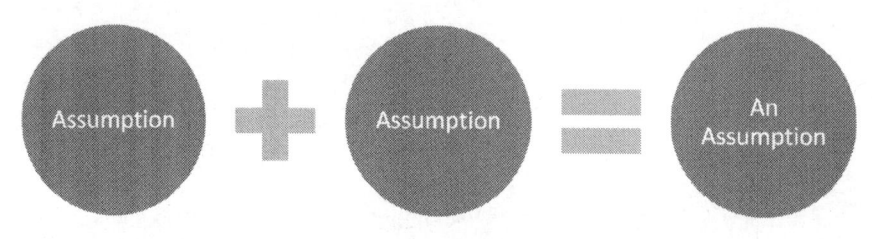

Assumption + Assumption = An Assumption

CHAPTER SEVENTEEN
CROE
Communication Rules Of Engagement

Good communication involves listening and talking, and these are what I call a few rules of engagement that will help you become a more effective communicator. I know this all sounds so elementary, but sometimes we forget that good communication involves being a good listener as well as talking. I would argue that listening is more important than talking. One of the most important elements of communication is to know your audience and your message.

- **Warmth and Attentiveness**: Most people don't have the time of day to really be nice to the next person. People today don't really talk to each other, but at each other. I always say it doesn't cost you anything to be nice to someone or even to say hello. There is nothing wrong with a genuine warm hello. Be warm and attentive, it's free. When you are doing business or just hanging out at a social event being warm and genuine is priceless.

- **Have a clear and effective message**: If you are going to say anything at all, then it should be as clear and as concise as possible. Make sure the person you are addressing understands exactly where you are coming from. No one wants to be confused about your intent or your message.

- **Always show that you are listening**: Communication is a dynamic, interactive process. Unless you show that you are listening, people will lose confidence in whatever it is they are saying, think you're not interested, and grind to a halt. You'll miss out on all the really interesting, meat and potatoes. So how do you show that you are listening? Some common and useful strategies include positive body language, making eye contact, repeating the message and providing engaging responses.

- **Use non-verbal methods of communication:** Think laterally. Think creatively. Support and enhance your message with non-verbal tools such as a diagram, prop, PowerPoint presentation or videos. Sometimes you need external communication tools to help illustrate your ideas.

- **Have a common understanding:** Show that you are on the same page, that you are really "getting" what is being said. Let the person know that you care enough to listen with your heart and your ears. Speak and respond when appropriate.

CHAPTER EIGHTEEN
EDKY
Everyone Doesn't Know You

I could put a dime in the meter right here. I consider myself to be a jokester and I like to have fun and play around with people. As a Major in the Army, not everyone knows that I have a silly side. If I show this side to you one time then I automatically assume that you get me. Well, that is not the case. It just means that you have encountered me for a brief moment in time, and you really don't know me at all. Okay, that leads me to my next story.

I was introduced to another Major at Fort Bragg. You know how people want to connect you with good people. When I met this Major she seemed nice at our first encounter. I made a few jokes and that was it. I saw this Major again about a week or two later. I recognized her at a distance about to get on the elevator. I ran to catch the elevator (what a mistake) and while on the elevator, I made a few jokes. The Major took my humor in the wrong way and what an awkward moment it became. I asked her if she remembered me and she said, "Who are you?" (So shallow) I said, "We met the other day." She just took it to another level and I don't even want to say anymore, but I said to myself "Everyone doesn't know you." I thought she remembered me and I thought I could joke around with her.

Relationships take time to build and people need time to get to know you. It's no fun going around telling people who you are when you should just allow them time to get to know you at their own pace. There are times when I want to say things that I don't think are offensive. I remind myself that these people don't know you, so watch what you say and how you say it. In time people will know you, just don't force it. That is an easy way to lose cool points. Its okay to want to be liked by others but it shouldn't be a priority, as the effort will drive you crazy. This chapter is definitely a chapter for me. This is something that I have to tell myself almost every day. No need to be offended just be aware.

Even if you don't feel like you are smart enough to be in the room there is a reason why you are there. Since you are there take advantage of the communication and people that surround you. It just might be beneficial to you and it may help you in your everyday life and your business. Get to know people and let them get to know you. Do not force feed yourself on people; you're worth more than that. In addition, realize that in this day and age you have to learn how to communicate with people who don't look like you, or have the same cultural background or the same beliefs or understanding that you may bring to the table.

Identify and list two people you thought knew you, but they really didn't know you this week.

1. _____
2. _____

Everyone Doesn't Know You

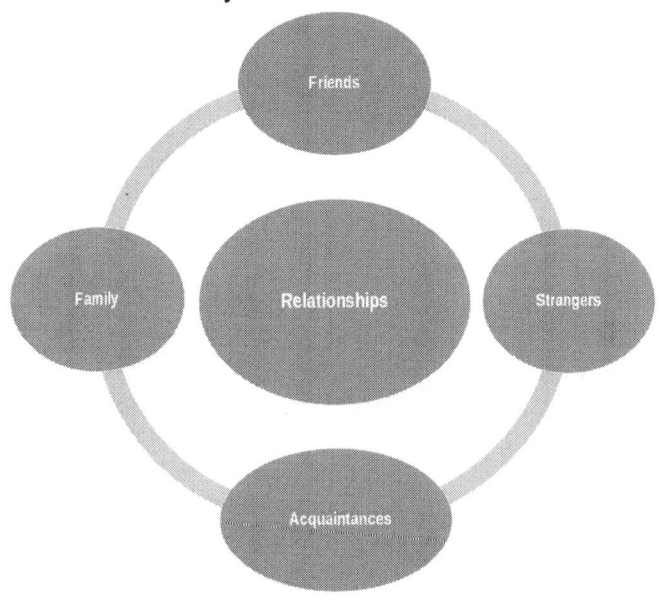

- Friends
- Family
- Relationships
- Strangers
- Acquaintances

CHAPTER NINETEEN
LOPT
Let Other People Talk

One thing I have learned in life is that most people have something to say, even if it's very little. People have an opinion about things, people, and life. In this chapter, the focus is about allowing others to get a word in.

Here is a situation. There are people who speak on a frequent basis; preachers come to mind (stay with me). On Sunday morning the preacher gets up to deliver his message. Sometimes the message is very powerful and people are deeply touched by the particular message. During the time of the sermon, there are people taking notes and writing things down. While doing so, some people have made up their mind that when the service is over, they are going to talk to the preacher about the powerful sermon they have just heard. There is nothing wrong with that. Most people will stand in line in order to shake the preacher's hand and tell him what a great sermon he has delivered and how they were personally touched. Okay, here comes the issue. Once the person reaches the preacher they decide to put a dime in the meter and hold a long conversation. However, there are 20 other people standing in line trying to speak with the same preacher. This is where consideration needs to kick in. You are not the only person who wants to talk to him. Let other people talk, move on; make an appointment if you need more time. There is a saying that, "there are times and places for everything." Don't get me wrong, it's in your right to talk to the preacher, however, allow other people to talk to him too. This was just one example. There are a host of others.

When you attend a conference and you hear a dynamic speaker you want to hone in on the speaker and tell them your life story and share what an impact they have just had on you. Again, there is nothing wrong with that. However, be assured you are not the only person who feels the same way. We should always consider and give way to the fact that other people want to talk and other people have something to say, just like you. I have seen this so many times! How rude would I be to say something like, "Hey that's enough, move on, make an appointment! There are other people waiting to say something!" I crack myself up! Just always try to consider the other person and be mindful that other people may feel exactly the same way you do.

Identify and list four people you just let talk this week.

1. _____
2. _____
3. _____
4. _____

Let Other People Talk

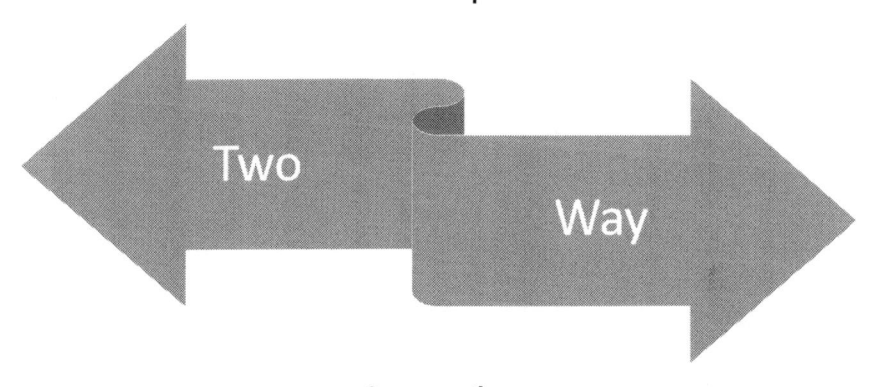

Two Way

Conversation

CHAPTER TWENTY
NWS
Network with Strangers

Most of us have always been told not to talk to strangers. For some of the most obvious reasons, we understand that talking to a stranger can be dangerous to our well-being. It is good advice, but I want to give a different kind of advice. When it comes to business and moving forward in life, my advice is to "network with strangers." Talk to a stranger who looks interesting. Not everyone you speak to wants to do you harm. There are some people who want to help you take your life and your business to the next level. You won't know they can help if you don't talk to them. Okay, a few ways to meet decent strangers is to attend networking events, join Chamber of Commerce organizations, and attend business mixers. Trust me these places are full of strangers who share a commonality of being successful and a willingness to help you climb to the next level of success.

    I remember when I was a young Captain and I was stationed at a unit in Los Angeles, California. There was a lady who worked with the Family Readiness Group. I hesitated to talk to her because I really didn't know her and I thought to myself how she can help me on my current quest. As time went on we spoke. Little by little and before you knew it, we were networking and exchanging ideas. As time passed she started inviting me to different events where I could help make a difference in the community. She noticed that I had a love for speaking and that I was a radio personality. Slowly, but surely she started to invite me to speak at different events it was through her that I achieved a certain amount of success in my life and business. Eventually, she got me to ride on the float at the Pasadena Tournament of Roses Parade. That was big deal for me. I look back and I think if I had never networked with her, I may not have gotten that opportunity. You never know what networking with strangers can do for you. I am not saying that all networking is good networking. Always network with caution and know that not every soul can be trusted and that sometimes people will waste your time and efforts. For the most part, if networking is a challenge to you, practice being good at it. Set a goal to attend at least two networking events a week. Networking with strangers is a two-way street. A guide to networking with strangers is to always look to see what you can give to that person. If the opportunity presents itself, take what they can give to you. Networking with strangers can also be the beginning of a beautiful friendship.

Identify and list three strangers you met and networked with this week.

1. _____
2. _____
3. _____

Network with Strangers

Stranger + Stranger = Possible future Friend

CHAPTER TWENTY-ONE

TCS

Toxic Communication Stinks

When I think of the word "toxic," I think of something that is dangerous, disgusting and harmful to my health and I want to stay as far away from it as possible. The first thing that comes to mind is a toxic waste site. Yuck! Well, there is a thing called toxic communication. I have heard it and it stinks. Even though I heard it, I smelled it too. I never knew you can smell with your eyes and ears. Wouldn't it be cool if you could smell toxic people a mile away approaching with their toxic communication? It might seem a little harsh, but some people are toxic and they may not even know it. These are a few toxic signs that people have and if you are one of them then you can recognize and make adjustments right now.

Have you ever received a compliment? Instead of saying thank you I appreciate it you say something negative. The person giving the compliment says: "that is a nice suit you have on". Your reply **"this is an old suit and it's too big for me. I lost weight I need to buy another one. I didn't have anything else to wear so I just grabbed this one."** All that noise when all you have to say is thank you. Sometimes people don't want to hear the extra conversation. Just answer the compliment. It may not seem toxic, but the person giving the compliment will be reluctant to give you a future compliment because now they know what to expect.

Another toxic conversation comes from those who feel like they aren't good enough or nobody would ever pick me. There is a long list of reasons why (or excuses) they aren't good enough for a new position, a good relationship, an education, a promotion, a slimmer body and the list goes on. I consider myself to be an extremely positive person and after a while, that kind of conversation can bring you down. It's a toxic yoke and it's hard to function with a yoke.

Here is another sign of a toxic communication. When people are having a negative conversation just like Double Dutch, there is someone who is ready to jump in and participate to add their own negative story, something bad that has happened to them. If the weather is bad then that equals a bad day. Talking about the leadership at work, and saying how incompetent they are. I guess that's why they are in a leadership position. Incompetence can carry you a long way. Some people start a sentence with the problem instead of the solution. Some people shoot down your ideas like Duck Hunt. Some people tell you that you will never make it or be anything. Okay you get the picture

It's not a sin to be happy. Some people leak internal poison in business and personal relationships and it affects everything that they do. Do you need to call poison control and clear out the toxins? The solution is to communicate empowering and uplifting messages to yourself and everyone you meet! You don't have to lie, but you don't have to crush a person's dreams.

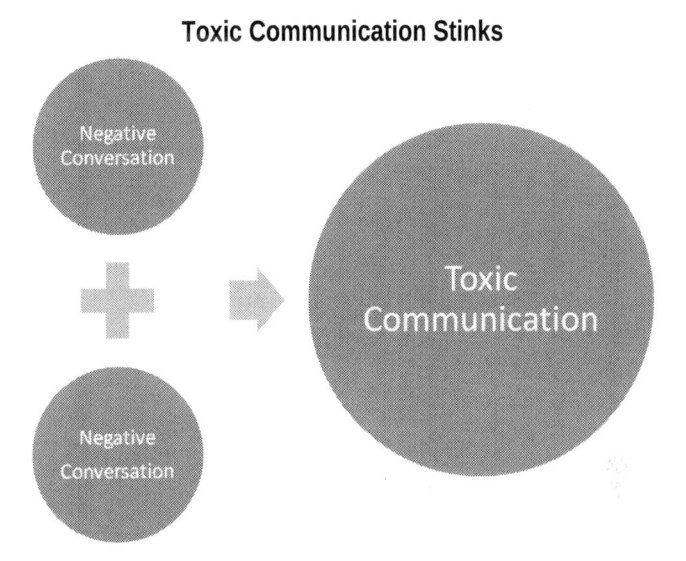

Toxic Communication Stinks

Negative Conversation + Negative Conversation → Toxic Communication

CHAPTER TWENTY-TWO

HOCAAT

Have One Conversation at a Time

I am sure most people can relate to this chapter. Have you ever met someone who talks to you and talks to someone else at the same time? I am not talking about a group conversation when there is a three-way conversation going. I am talking about a time when you are in the middle of your climax sentence and the person you are talking to starts talking to someone else while they were supposed to be talking to you. If you really pay close attention, you will see it more often than you realize. Okay, here are some examples. I was talking to a few Soldiers trying to explain a project we were working on. As I was talking to the more senior Soldier right in the middle of my sentence he starts talking to another Soldier. I thought to myself "I am still talking" how rude!" This happens every single time I talk to this particular Soldier. He has a thought and instead of writing it down or waiting until I am done, he starts talking. This makes me feel like he is not really interested in what I am saying. I am the type who doesn't like wasting my time. Talking to a person who doesn't want to hear me, definitely translates to a waste of my time and energy.

Okay, this will cut into a previous chapter, Chapter Nineteen, "Let Other People Talk."

I can understand if someone is passing by and that person says, "hello," and the person turns to speak to the individual who is passing by and says, "hello" in return. I call that an exemption to the interruption rule. Sometimes you have to know that other people will pass by and say hello, don't get mad just know that it happens. When you are talking to someone concentrate on your conversation with that person and that person only. If you have something to say or if you want to talk to someone else while in conversation then say, "Excuse me" or "May we continue this conversation later?" You are not the only one who has time on the clock. Consider that other people could spend their time talking to someone else and not someone as rude as you.

Some grown people have Attention Deficit Disorder (ADD). If you can help yourself, try to give the person talking to you the respect they deserve and don't interrupt them. Another example is when I am talking to someone on the phone that has children; this might be the worst situation. When you say, "hello" and start to get into the conversation you hear "Hey, put that down" or "Hey stop that, I am on the phone." You immediately know that the person on the phone is not talking to you. I understand that sometimes that type of conversation can't be helped. Kids will cut up once you get on the phone. I would say go to another room, but then you have kids unattended and that won't work. Now that I think about it most people have ADD because there is always something or someone in the background impeding on their attention. Simple words can be used, "Let me call you back," "Can you talk at a later time" or "I am distracted, I will call you back."

Have One Conversation at a Time

- I am talking to my friend
- My kids just walked in the door
- I am trying to send an email
- I am trying to send you a text
- My husand is talking to me

Who are you talking to?

CHAPTER TWENTY-THREE
DLTP
Don't Lie To People

We have all heard that honesty is the best policy. I am a very straightforward person and believe it or not, sometimes it's hard for me to be honest. It's not that I can't be honest; it's just that some people can't take pure honesty. That is one thing I have learned in my life. No matter how gentle you are in telling someone the truth they will still get mad, angry and revengeful towards you. Experience is a good teacher; it takes someone like me to know. No matter what the situation or circumstance don't lie to people. There are a few social arguments that say it's okay to lie and it depends on the situation. I see that as a worldview. There is a much higher power that says "thou shall not lie" that is the view I listen to and respect more than the world's view. I have a twin sister and she is developing a t-shirt line. She showed me her logo and I thought it was nice. She came up with a second logo and the logo was a woman with her panties and bra. My first reaction was *that doesn't look good for a woman to wear on a T-shirt, a woman in her underwear.* It reminded me of a playboy bunny t-shirt. Now, this was my view, not the world's view. Most of the designs my sister comes up with I love, but this one was a little too much for me personally. The fact is that I didn't lie to her. If she chooses to continue to wear the t-shirt then that is her choice. Sometimes it's harder to tell the family the truth, but family members make for good practice for telling the truth to the world.

One thing about telling a lie is that you will not always remember the lie. You would have to rehearse the lie and always remember it. The truth is the truth; you can't forget what is real. If you are trying to do business with a person or get that promotion the best thing to do is to be you. Don't makeup complements and say things that you really don't mean in order to get on someone's good side. If a man is not attractive don't tell him he is handsome, because you want to do business with him. You don't have to say anything extra, just make sure you promise only what you can deliver. Not need to go overboard with a lie in order to seal the deal. The truth will do that for you.

One practice that I have implemented in my life is that if a person is going to lie about something big or small, I tell them not to include me or tell me about it. I can't be on the same page with something that I don't believe in. You can lie, but please don't ask me to. You can't hold me to your standards. I have seen people get mad at others because they didn't want to lie for them. I tell Soldiers and people who work under me to let me know what's going on because if I don't know where they are or what they are up to then I will not make something up. My least favorite response is *"I don't know"* even though I don't like that response I will use it instead of telling a lie. The "I don't' know" would be the truth. Believe it or not, it's much worst when a person finds out that you lied to them. Just don't lie to people.

MY LITTLE BLACK "A" BOOK

CHAPTER TWENTY-FOUR

PATD

Pay Attention to Details

This is one that is near and dear to my heart and that has been instilled in me for a long time. There are times in everyone's life when they leave something out or they forget to include something in a situation. Sometimes in a fast paced-work environment, we all get busy and a steady flow of continuous work makes it challenging to include every detail of the job or task we are handling. Sometimes overlooking details can cost you a lot in one way or another. It can cost you money, time or even a job or client. It's detrimental to you or maybe other people who will be directly affected by your lack of attention to details. Paying attention to detail is a key factor in effective communication. We all can improve our overall attention to detail by using a few strategic planning and communication techniques.

Okay, this is where it gets exciting because now we can tie a few elements together that have already been mentioned in this book. When it comes to effective communication you have to cut out distractions, listen and write things down during the conversation. It might not hurt to record the conversation with permission and go back and listen to it later. Here is what that looks like.

You are a caterer and you have a meeting with a client. The only place for you to meet the client is in your restaurant. This is a big deal so you don't want to mess up the opportunity. The client meets you at the restaurant that can sometimes get really noisy. You decide to have the meeting in your closed-door office. You tell your staff not to disturb you and you turn off your cell phone. Before you get started you ask the client if you can record the session. The client tells you what they want and what type of food they want. You are listening, taking notes and asking questions. You listen to every word and take copious notes. You don't remember everything that was said but you know you recorded the meeting. This is a good workflow. You have to be engaged and you have to "pay attention to detail". The meeting is over. A few hours later the client calls you back and you are really busy. The client tells you that they are allergic to peanuts and you say okay got it. That is a small big detail. You were so busy that you didn't write it down. The day of the event comes and you forgot the small detail that the client couldn't eat peanuts. One of your staff crushes peanuts and puts it in one of the dishes. You realize that you forgot that one little big detail because you were extremely busy when the information was given to you. This mistake may have cost the client their life but instead, they were rushed to the hospital and survived. Pay attention to detail. It's important to listen, take present notes, future notes and record with permission if necessary.

CHAPTER TWENTY-FIVE

APYCS

Always Practice Your Communication Skills

Now that you have a few communication acronyms in your tool bag this one will be the icing on the cake. We have all heard the expression, "Practice makes Perfect." You always have to practice so that your communication is more perfect today than it was yesterday. Rome was not built in a day and it will take time for you to learn how to effectively communicate. There are a few things that I will stress in this chapter. Things to remember when you are having a conversation with someone. Make sure you are speaking clearly and that people can understand what you are saying. Having a good understanding is important so that people will understand where you are coming from. If you are not the best communicator if you don't always speak clearly than take an elocution class. It will help you with your pronunciation. People want to understand what you are saying.

    Listening again is an important element of communication. Do take the time to sit in a quiet room and just be silent, don't say anything, just listen. We know you can talk, but can you listen as well? Without interjecting, practice listening to people. Tell the person you are talking to what you are doing and let them remind you that you are just there to listen.

    Taking notes when you are talking to people will avoid forgetting something they have said. There might be a point you want to make instead of interrupting, write down the comment the person made during the conversation and when it's your turn bring it up and make your comment.

    Communication is not always easy even under the best of circumstances, but it's something that is necessary and it's something we do every single day of our lives. Effective communication can serve you well; you have to practice the skills of communication as it will help you in your relationships with, family, friends, clients, and strangers. Effective communication can open more doors for you and create great life opportunities that you might not have otherwise had. People like to be heard and listened to. The goal is to be good at both. Mastering effective communication with conversation and listening will set you apart and put you in a league of your own. Keep these acronyms close and use them before you have your next conversation. Thanks for reading my book.

Identify and list three ways you will try to be more effective in your communication this week.

1. _____
2. _____
3. _____

Always Practice Your Communication Skills

Practice Good Communication

Be Cautious in your Communication

Don't Stop Practicing your Communication

ACRONYM REFERENCES

CCC = The 3 C's of Communication Communicate, Collaborate, Commit

WAIT = Why Am I Talking,

BLUF = Bottom Line Up Front

SEE = Speak Educate Excite

LJASU = Just Listen and Shut Up

ALF = Always Listen First

CUT = Communication under Trust

DIP = Don't Interrupt People

LTO = Listen to Opinions

PATAPBL = Pay attention to a Person's Body Language

DAWAC = Don't Argue with a Client

CDT = Call Don't Text

INAM = It's Not About Me

LFO = Learn from Others

LWYH = Listen With Your Heart

YLBL = You learn By Listening

DAYKTO = Don't Assume You Know the Outcome

CROE = Communication Rule of Engagement

EDKY = Everyone Doesn't Know You

STC = Share the Conversation

NWS = Network with Strangers

TCS = Toxic Communication Stinks

HOCAAT = Have One Conversation at a Time

DLTP = Don't Lie to People

PATD = Pay Attention to Details

APYCS = Always Practice your Communication Skills

MY LITTLE BLACK "A" BOOK
Communication Acronyms
Effective Communication in a Noisy World
By Major Lynette Jones
Available on Amazon Kindle and in Hard Copy

To book Ms. Lynette Jones for your next speaking event
Please Contact
IRENE MINK
NEW DAY TALK RADIO MEDIA CENTER
310.594.5001 or 310.433-6700

New Day Talk Radio Where Every Day Is A New Day!
www.newdaytalkradio.com
ISBN: 9781980938262

Made in the USA
Middletown, DE
20 May 2018